# UNIVERSITY

## A Survival Guide

Need
— 2 —
Know

Anne
Coates

D1344796

First published in Great Britain in 2009 by
**Need2Know**
Remus House
Coltsfoot Drive
Peterborough
PE2 9JX
Telephone 01733 898103
Fax 01733 313524
www.need2knowbooks.co.uk

Need2Know is an imprint of Forward Press Ltd.
www.forwardpress.co.uk
SB ISBN 978-1-86144-072-3
Cover photograph: Jupiter Images

# Contents

# Introduction

*University – A Survival Guide* follows on from my first book in this imprint, *Applying to University – The Essential Guide* which gives a step-by-step guide to finding the right university and advice on how to make your application successful. This book takes you to the next stage.

Leaving home and going to university is one of the most exciting and frightening challenges you can face. It might be the first time you have lived away from home, and the thought of all that freedom without a parent nagging you to tidy your room or monitor what time you come home is heady indeed. It's almost as intoxicating as all the alcohol you plan to get through in freshers' week!

Yet there are bound to be questions, fears and worries in the back of your mind. This book sets out to address all these issues, like what do you need to take with you? Supposing you feel homesick? What if you don't make friends? Where can you get emergency contraception? It will take you through the entire process: from leaving home and moving in to making the most of freshers' week and familiarising yourself with your department.

There are also chapters on keeping healthy, what to eat (and what not to!), sex and relationships, how to sort out your finances and save money, how to prepare for exams and how to settle into your student accommodation.

Current students and new graduates share their experiences and tips, as well as revealing their own uncertainties.

I hope reading this book will encourage you to take a broader outlook on your life as a student and think about the future. Planning what you do to earn money both during term time and the holiday periods can improve your possibilities for employment as a graduate, as can volunteering and joining clubs and societies.

The university experience is a way of life and this book will help you to live it to the full.

# Chapter One

# Forward Planning

Going to university is a huge step for most young people and you may be living away from home for the first time, enjoying an independence you're unlikely to have had before. This can be an exciting and welcome transition, marking your entry into adulthood, but for some it can be daunting and, let's face it, a bit scary!

Miguel de Cervantes once said, 'To be prepared is half the victory.' This is very true.

Forward planning can help take a lot of the stress out of any situation, so don't leave things to chance. Sort out as much as you can before you actually leave home. That way you will be able to concentrate on enjoying the university experience.

## Documents

Read every letter, document or email you get from UCAS and the university you are going to carefully. It's amazing what you can miss when just giving a cursory glance, and the last thing you want to do is to turn up without having followed all the instructions you've been given. If you don't understand something – ask! If necessary, phone the person who sent the letter and ask them for clarification. You won't make yourself look silly by asking a question, but you will if you forget to take the correct documentation with you!

'Forward planning can help take a lot of the stress out of any situation, so don't leave things to chance. Sort out as much as you can before you actually leave home.'

# Finances

'I (Mum) managed to get most things sorted before I left, so it was okay. But towards the end of the first year the student loans company sends you reminders to go online and fill in this form (update details of address, etc) so you get your loan renewed in time for next year. I missed the deadline by a week or so, so it isn't that strict but I know some people who completely forgot and didn't get a loan for the first two months of their second year. The form takes two minutes, so there's no reason not to fill it in!' Joel.

'I left changing my bank account to the last minute and it caused no end of problems, mostly due to the bank's inefficiency. They sent my debit card to my home address, causing me problems in my first week as I couldn't use my old card.' Ellen.

> 'I left changing my bank account to the last minute and it caused no end of problems, mostly due to the bank's inefficiency. They sent my debit card to my home address, causing me problems in my first week as I couldn't use my old card.'

## Choosing where to bank

Young people tend to bank where their parents do, but there is no reason to do this. Your parents may not be getting the best deal or account for them, so this is an opportune time to shop around and see what is on offer. If you have previously had a young person's bank account, you will need to change this as it will not give you an overdraft facility or cheque book. If you have been working before going on to study, you may already have an account with a bank. You would be wise to change to a student account to take advantage of free banking and interest-free or low interest overdafts.

Each of the big banks will offer something to tempt students, for example a three year student railcard, music vouchers or a higher overdraft limit. However, don't get sucked in by the 'freebie' – what you need to consider is the amount of overdraft you may need and the lowest interest rates.

Each year, money saving expert Martin Lewis produces an overview of what banks are offering students and where to look. This is usually published on his website in July or August and is well worth studying as Martin has made it his mission in life to save people money. You will also find lots of other valuable financial advice on the site including travel offers and two for one restaurant deals. Visit www.moneysavingexpert.com and save it in your favourites so you can keep up-to-date with what's on offer.

As with most things, one type of bank account may be suitable for one student but less so for another. For instance, if you have decided to go to your local university or if you have a car, you may have little use for a student railcard. If having access to an overdraft facility is important to you then you need to have the best deal. Martin sets this out in a way that is easily understood and is very good at organising student banking.

Whichever bank you go with, you need to have your bank account sorted before you get to university so that any loan or bursary can be paid to you on time. You'll also be asked to set up a direct debit to pay your accommodation costs.

It is important that you have a debit card and cheque book, although you probably won't have to write cheques very often as you can pay for most items or bills with your debit card. You may also be offered a credit card (see below).

Make sure you keep your cheque book and debit card in a safe place (but not together as the debit card also acts as a cheque guarantee). Remember, don't write down your PIN number where it can be found – learn it by heart!

## Credit cards

Credit cards get a bad press but, used sensibly, they are a useful tool in financial planning. If you get one, you will not get a high credit limit – probably around £500 to £1000. However, you shouldn't think of this as extra spending money or as a top up to your loan but rather as emergency money and a means of paying for things in a safe way. Any purchases made which cost over £100 (and under £30,000!) are covered under Section 75 of the Consumer Credit Act 1974. This means if the product isn't fit for purpose or doesn't arrive, or the company goes into liquidation, the credit card company will reimburse you. This is your insurance when making large purchases and can be very useful.

If you are very disciplined, you could make most of your purchases (for food and travel, etc) by credit card and enjoy the free credit time. For this to work you must pay off your credit card bill in full every month so that you don't incur interest charges.

'Whichever bank you go with, you need to have your bank account sorted before you get to university so that any loan or bursary can be paid to you on time.'

Another reason for having a credit card while you are a student is that you begin a 'credit history'. One recent graduate was turned down for a credit card even though she was in full time employment as there were no records of how she had previously managed her finances. However, her sister took out a credit card as a student and had no such problems when she graduated.

## Banking online

Setting up your account online is simple and will give you 24-hour access to your bank. You can then pay bills, transfer cash and check that money has been paid into your account at the click of a mouse.

# Insurance

Another thing that must be done is to insure all your belongings against loss, accidental damage and theft. The statistics about students being burgled in their first terms are quite alarming. Just imagine if you had your computer or sound system stolen and didn't have the money to replace it!

Before you buy your own insurance, check that you aren't covered on your parents' home insurance policy – you may be lucky and find that some of your personal belongings are already covered. It is also wise to be wary of mobile phone insurance. It's costly and there are often lots of terms and conditions attached to the policy – for example, you may not be covered if you are using your mobile but are out of the country for more than a month.

Endsleigh is the only company recommended by the National Union of Students (NUS) and offers a comprehensive policy that is easy to access online (many universities also have an Endsleigh office on campus). You will also find your university and halls of residence listed so you can get an immediate quote for the cover you need. There are different costs for various types of accommodation and areas, as well as different items. For example, you may pay more to cover a laptop than a desktop computer. Endsleigh also provide holiday insurance that is competitively priced. Visit www.endsleigh. co.uk to find out more.

# Accommodation

'Bring things (posters, pictures, mirrors, etc) for your room that will make you feel more at home and less like you are moving into a room that is alien to you. Ensure you know what the university provides in your room so you are not missing anything – for example, I need a bedside table.' Libby, Manchester.

'My son didn't get the accommodation form signed and sent in time so he had to send it by special delivery. In the meantime he received an email asking if he still wanted the room! It worked out okay, but it was all very stressful.' Laura.

You will have applied for your accommodation when you were offered a conditional – or if you already had your A level results, an unconditional – university place. You may not have been allocated your first choice but don't despair as it is possible to change if you're really unhappy.

Check out your university website for the latest information on the various types of accommodation it offers, plus advice and tips from current students. Most have a virtual tour facility and will usually list what the rooms come with.

Carefully read all the documentation you receive from the university. You will probably have to complete a form saying how the cost of your residence will be met. If your parents are paying, they will be offered schemes by which to do this – for example, termly or monthly. If you are paying from your student loan, you will have to fill in this part of the form with details of your bank account. You will also have to send a deposit by cheque and sign an agreement. Make sure you do this by the date you are given or you could lose your room.

**'When you are thinking about what to take with you, think of things that will make you feel at home.'**

The first thing to remember is that your accommodation won't be anything like home. It will probably seem quite bleak when you arrive – student residences are not luxurious and there are few home comforts. When you are thinking about what to take with you, think of things that will make you feel at home.

# Online before you go

'I wish I had registered and applied for my optional module before I left home as everything was so new and unnerving at university that I was very unsure of what to choose.' Libby.

Once you get your results and confirmation of your place, you will be asked to complete certain formalities online. This is usually self-explanatory and easy to do, but if you have any problems or questions, ring the appropriate helpline. You will find a list of numbers in the documentation you have received from the university or on their website. The university staff are there to talk you through any problems you may have. They have probably heard every enquiry before and won't think you're being silly!

You can also join any fresher forum that interests you and begin to make friends before you actually start university.

Usually you can find online (or be sent by post) the times when you have introductory lectures and meetings with your department. Put these in your diary as soon as you get them. If you're not used to keeping a diary, now is the time to start. Buy an academic diary so that it starts in September and sees you through the first year. Don't panic if you aren't given all the details about your course before term starts – some universities don't provide them until the first week.

'You may be asked to read certain books before you actually arrive at university. Make sure you get hold of these and don't leave reading them until the last minute!'

## Reading list

You may be asked to read certain books before you actually arrive at university. Make sure you get hold of these and don't leave reading them until the last minute!

When buying books, check out all the websites that offer good deals like www.amazon.com and www.play.com. You may find that you can buy second-hand copies of the books you need at a bargain price. However, be aware that some second-hand books are as expensive as new copies as people can charge for postage and packaging, which may greatly increase the price. Another good way of finding cheap books is to join the Facebook group for your university. You may find second year students selling their books there. If you don't need a book before you arrive, arrange to collect it at the beginning of term or else postal charges may make it just as expensive as buying one new.

Alternatively, wait until you arrive at university and check out all the second-hand bookshops for the titles you need.

# What you need to take with you

The following lists will help you remember the basics. You might like to make a copy of them so that if anyone wants to buy you something to go away with they can give you something useful. Give the list to your parents – family members and friends might ask them for leaving present ideas!

## Basic list

- Pillows, duvet, sheets and pillow-cases (you will need at least two sets so you can change your bed without having to wait for the washing to dry!), plus a mattress protector which some halls insist on.

- Bath towels, medium sized towels and hand towels – at least two of each.

- Clothes and shoes (remember as you leave for your first term that the weather may still be very warm, so think winter when you're choosing clothes to take). A dressing gown will be useful – don't forget that you're likely to be sharing a flat with both sexes!

- Toiletries – if your parents are offering to do a 'big shop' for you, say yes and stock up. You'll be amazed at how expensive everything seems once you are on a limited budget! Don't forget to pack toilet rolls!

- Books and stationery, including memory sticks, blank CDs, post-it notes, scissors, a stapler and a hole punch, as well as the usual pens, pencils and highlighters.

- Computer and printer.

- Sports equipment and clothes, including swimsuit/trunks.

- An address book for numbers and addresses just in case you lose your mobile phone. If you use this facility on your computer, make sure you back it up somewhere else.

- Mobile phone and camera – don't forget the chargers!

- Music/iPod/MP3 Player, plus speakers and a charger.

- DVDs as they are a good way to relax and share with flatmates, and help to break the ice – they may hate your selection but it's a good conversation topic!

- A pack of playing cards or a favourite board game – great for a cheap evening in with flatmates.

- A first aid box containing replacement salts (for diarrhoea and vomiting), painkillers, plasters and antiseptic cream.

- Ear plugs for when you need an early night and your flatmates don't!

- A sewing kit including needles, thread and scissors.

- A bedside lamp.

## Don't forget

If you wear contact lenses or glasses, make sure you have your prescription with you just in case you lose or break them.

If you have to take regular medication, make sure you have enough with you.

## If in a self-catering hall you will need:

- Mugs, plates, cutlery, bowls and glasses.

- Cooking utensils – a minimum of one frying pan and one saucepan plus a tin or casserole dish for the oven.

- Tin opener.

- Corkscrew and bottle opener.

- Cheese grater.

- Tupperware containers.

- Tea towels.

- Knives to prepare food and a fish slice.

- Vegetable peeler.

'Don't buy every single kitchen utensil you can think of, because chances are someone else will as well and you'll end up with 25 wooden spoons. You can buy anything else you need in the first week or so.'

Joel.

- Colander and/or a sieve.
- Wooden spoon.
- Oven gloves.
- A padlock for your food cupboard.

You do not need to buy or take items like toasters with you. Wait to see what's actually provided in your kitchen and if you really need anything you can make a group purchase. See *Student Cookbook – Healthy Eating* (Need2Know) for a list of cupboard essentials.

## Getting there

If you are driving, plan your route in advance and get a map of the area that your hall is in. Remember, the journey is likely to be stressful for your parents as well (they'll be worrying about leaving you, how you'll cope, what your flatmates are like and so on), so the last thing you need is to get lost. A good investment is to buy an A-Z map of the city or town you are going to.

If you are travelling by train or coach, book your tickets early for the best deal. You could even consider sending on your luggage (see overleaf). See the help list at the back for some useful websites you can visit when buying tickets for travel.

## Packing

If you are being taken to university by car, you'll be able to load your belongings into black bags and boxes. But remember, you'll need a weekend bag and a fair sized suitcase or backpack for when you come home for the holiday periods.

If you've bought a starter pack of crockery, leave it in its packaging as it's less likely to break en route.

Remember to take plenty of hangers with you – you may have more hanging space than drawers.

'As we drove up the M1 we saw car after car that was obviously taking a student to university – the black bag syndrome gave them away!'

Isabel.

## Sending luggage

If you are not being taken to university by car (or even if you are), you might like to consider sending your luggage via a door-to-door delivery service. This may be especially useful when you are coming home and returning from the Christmas and Easter holidays.

Booking the service is very simple via www.carrymyluggage.com (click on 'bookings' and then follow the prompts on screen) and you can arrange for a collection with just 24 hours notice. Collection times are Monday to Friday from 9am to 5pm, with deliveries made the next business day by 4pm.

For the Smarter Students service, make an online booking at www.firstluggage.com. You need to book two to three days in advance, but for UK to UK collections and deliveries there is an option to request next day and weekend delivery.

# Checklist of all the things you need to have done:

- Set up a student bank account.

- Organised insurance cover for your personal belongings.

- Applied for a student railcard.

- Completed and signed forms for halls and your course.

- Made lists of all the things you need to take with you and/or need to buy.

- Bought an address book and filled it in.

- Given your new address to everyone – it's still nice to receive post rather than emails, and your birthday may be during term time!

- Arranged for a luggage collection service if necessary.

- Booked a train ticket if appropriate.

# Summing Up

There are lots of things you can do (and should do) during the summer before you go to university. Sorting out your bank account is a must if you don't want to have problems in your first weeks.

Being prepared in other ways will also make the period less stressful. Having a list of what you need to take with you (and not leaving everything to the last minute) will make you feel more in control of any situation.

It is imperative that you read all the information you get from your university carefully so that you make any response within the allotted time. Don't ignore letters and make sure you check your emails. Remember that the university is dealing with thousands of students and has a time frame for allocating rooms and making sure all the places on courses are filled. If they don't hear from you, they may assume you no longer need your room.

If you've been given a book list, get the books and start reading. Very often, universities recommend books on how to study and get the most from your course. This is the time to read them!

'It is imperative that you read all the information you get from your university carefully so that you make any response within the allotted time. Don't ignore letters and make sure you check your emails.'

# Chapter Two
## Freshers' Week

'Go to all of the events in freshers' week, even if you are tired. You will regret missing out on time with your new friends once the work starts piling up! The work they set you or classes you need to attend in freshers' week are only tasters, so don't get worried or anxious about them.' Libby.

'Don't spend £20 signing up to loads of clubs or societies that you'll never actually go to. Don't go too mental in the first few days either because you'll feel exhausted for the rest of the week and will miss out. Get as many vouchers as you can – I'm still using them now in the third year! And if not, you can return to the freshers' fare in the second and third year to collect more.' Joel.

'University is what you make it. It's all down to you being open-minded and positive. Everyone gets freshers' flu – you may as well accept it. I'd say take Lemsips and paracetamol and try to eat well so you can keep your energy up. But it's inevitable after freshers' week that you're going to be unwell. Just be prepared for it and see it as part of the experience.' Jane.

This is the big week! A time to find out what university life has in store for you and a time to make friends and contacts. It will be a whirlwind of experiences, so try not to overindulge on alcohol so you remember at least some of it!

'When you arrive and move into your room, leave the door ajar. That way people will know you are there and will pop in and say hello.'
Kathryn.

## Arriving

'The best advice I was given was just to be myself and enjoy the experience. I think university can be a way of reinventing yourself or finding yourself again if you're a bit lost. Also, if you're in self-catered accommodation, remember that getting on with your flatmates is a bonus, not a necessity. There are plenty more people out there for you to meet.' Jane.

When my daughter and I arrived at Manchester, it was like a military operation, with security staff directing cars to relevant parking spaces and giving you half an hour to unload your belongings before moving on to a longer-stay car park. It was like organised chaos and, thank goodness, it wasn't raining!

Make sure you have all the relevant documentation you need with you. Have it in a folder that's easy to get to so you're not searching through bags at what is a stressful time, especially if you've had a long journey. Once you get your keys, make sure you look after them – it will cost a small fortune to have them replaced if they are lost.

You'll probably take one look at your room and your heart will sink. Don't worry – it will look so much better once you've unpacked and put your mark on it. If your parents are hanging around for a while, make use of them. You can rearrange anything afterwards but let them help you unpack, hang up your clothes, make up your bed and get suitcases and bags stowed away. Immediately your room will look more inviting.

'This is the time to start to get to know your flatmates and the layout of your halls of residence. So give your parents a hug, plaster a smile on your face and wave them off.'

## Saying goodbye

Discuss in advance with your parents how long they are going to stay. It should be long enough for you to unpack and perhaps do a supermarket shop if you are self-catering. Don't plan to have a meal with them – however tempting. This is the time to start getting to know your flatmates and the layout of your halls of residence. So give your parents a hug, plaster a smile on your face and wave them off.

# Internet connection

Get your Internet connection sorted as soon as possible – you'll want to be in touch with your friends and you'll need to check in with your department. You will also be given a university email address that you should check regularly for any messages from your tutors. You may have to buy a cable to connect to the Internet – during freshers' week there will be stalls selling the necessary items you need to buy. There will also be an IT office on campus if you have any problems setting everything up.

# Library card and admin

During freshers' week there's a whole lot of admin to do, so make sure you are organised. For instance, you will need a library card for which your photo will be taken. This is free but beware of losing it as replacements may cost more than you think.

Registering may take a while but it has to be done and you need your university card.

You will also receive information about registering with a doctor and dentist – see chapter 6 for further details.

# Checking courses and options

'Do not choose a course because you like the sound of it or because "everyone else is doing it". Choose something you enjoy and that fits with your schedule – especially a subject that coincides with days you are already in uni – a day when you don't have to go in is always welcome!' Libby.

'We had a meeting with tutors and advisors for choosing our elective modules. I found that the first formal meeting terrified me because it all became so serious. It was my first and only "freak out" but you get over it and realise that it's not nearly as bad as you thought. The biggest change is that unlike school you're not spoon-fed. You are expected to organise things on your own. It's just a case of getting yourself into a good rhythm.' Jane.

During your first week you will have introductory lectures in your department and will probably be given tours of libraries and rooms. It will seem like a lot of information to take in, so make notes or take photos as a memory aid.

# Sorting local travel

Some students are given free bus passes for the first week. This gives you the opportunity to work out the best routes for where you need or want to be (and remember how different places look in the dark). Find out about last buses and

'Registering may take a while but it has to be done and you need your university card.'

night services. Check these with the student union, city council or university website. There may also be some sort of shuttle service between the university and the city centre which is funded by the university.

The Stagecoach Unirider scheme allows cheap travel within certain cities (check the website www.buymyunirider.com to see if it is available for you). It may work out cheaper to buy an annual or termly ticket rather than a weekly bus pass.

## Making friends

'If you are living in a nice region of the country like Devon or Yorkshire, then befriend someone with a car and get out at the weekends and make the most of it.' Guy.

Try not to make instant judgments about the other students you are sharing with – remember, you are all in a strange and new situation and everyone reacts differently in different circumstances. The show-off may actually be shy, while the one who looks timid may be sizing up the situation before showing their true colours. Be open-minded and remember to smile even if you're feeling overwhelmed.

## Homesickness

'Do not phone home too often. Throw yourself into as many things as possible, even if it is just going to the pub with your new flatmates! This prevents you from having time alone to worry or miss family and friends from home.' Libby.

'I think you have to find a strategy for homesickness that works for you – either talking to family at home regularly or saying you won't talk to them for a few weeks. Having been travelling, I don't find homesickness to be a problem at all, but to those that do I think they should persevere, not worry about things on their own and keep going because they'll regret it and miss out if they don't. You have to learn to be away from home some time and university is one of the best and most enjoyable ways to do it.' Jane.

Even if you thought you would never miss your home or family, the chances are you'll feel homesick at some time or another. Don't worry as it happens to everyone, even if they don't admit to it.

Going to university is a huge upheaval and you may be away from everyone and everything familiar to you, so there are bound to be moments when you feel lost and out of your depth. Don't panic. Try talking to your new friends or even your old ones – they may be experiencing the same feelings.

## Loneliness

Everyone feels lonely at some time or another. You can even feel lonely in a crowd, especially if you feel that you don't fit in. However, it may be that your flatmates are feeling lonely and a bit scared as well but are too embarrassed or shy to talk about it.

One of the questions new students often ask themselves is 'what if I don't make any friends?' Perhaps this sounds familiar to you. Just ask yourself 'do I have friends now?' Of course you do, so the likelihood is that you'll be able to make new friends.

It may be that it takes you longer to feel at ease with new acquaintances, which isn't necessarily a bad thing. Perhaps you are just more discerning! Don't feel that you have to do things you're not comfortable with.

If you're feeling shy, go for really easy ice breakers like 'I'm making a coffee, would you like one?', or hand round biscuits (note to parents: buy a big tin of assorted biscuits!).

You should sign up for at least one club or activity that really interests you. That way you are bound to meet like-minded people and increase your circle of friends. It's always good to have friends who are neither on your course or sharing your halls so you've always got an escape route if things get too much.

Try not to think about dashing home for the weekend or going off to see friends at another university. If you do this too early on, you'll miss opportunities to make friends and socialise. However, if you're feeling really lonely, please share your thoughts with someone. Check the help list at the end of this book for a list of places you can ring for a chat. You can also contact your personal tutor

'Even if you thought you would never miss your home or family, the chances are you'll feel homesick at some time or another. Don't worry as it happens to everyone, even if they don't admit to it.'

or visit one of the university chaplains – you don't have to share their religion and they are professional people trained to listen and counsel. They are used to students and the problems they can encounter.

# Partying

Go for it – you're only a fresher once. People don't usually regret the things they've done but rather what they didn't do. This week is for maximum socialising. A word of caution though – you do want to remember the people you've met and the things you've done, so don't drink so much alcohol that your memory is wiped out. See chapter 6 for more advice on drinking.

'Take an old school shirt and a tie – really comes in useful for fancy dress.'

Olie.

Lots of parties will be fancy dress – swap clothes and ideas with friends and flatmates. If you haven't brought anything with you, seek out local charity shops. If you're a guy, befriend a similar sized girl or one who will share her make-up! Be imaginative and innovative in interpreting themes – always a good talking point with people you don't know yet.

## Freshers' fair

All the clubs and societies set up their stalls at the freshers' fair and try to entice you to join them. This is a really good time to try out something you've always wanted to do – it will be much cheaper than at any other time in your life, plus you'll actually have the time to enjoy it! So if you've hankered after clay pigeon shooting – go for it. You'll also be able to meet second and third year students who will be able to give you advice on all sorts of things – from the most useful books to the best pubs! If you join a club or society and don't like it, you're not obliged to keep attending.

## Freshers' ball

Make sure you go the freshers' ball! Whatever you do, this is one not to miss. Check out the dress code (it could be fancy dress) and have a ball!

## Top tips for staying safe during freshers' week

- Try not to be on your own walking back from somewhere in the dark.

- Work out your route to and from a place beforehand.

- Girls – wear sensible shoes that you can walk quickly in and take party shoes or high heels with you to change when you get there.

- When you are walking along the pavement, walk facing the traffic so that a car won't be able to pull up alongside you or kerb crawl.

- Have the number of a reliable cab service in your mobile (student unions can often recommend taxi services).

- Keep some emergency cash on you in case you need a cab.

- Swap phone numbers with your flatmates – you don't know when you may need to contact someone.

- Never get into a minicab that you haven't pre-booked. It is illegal for minicabs to pick up passengers without booking. They may be operating without a licence or proper insurance.

'Make sure you go the freshers' ball! Whatever you do, this is one not to miss. Check out the dress code (it could be fancy dress) and have a ball!'

# Summing Up

Freshers' week is a fantastic start to university life. It's goodbye Mum and Dad, hello new friends! But that doesn't mean that you won't feel homesick or lonely and need strategies for coping.

Everyone should try to sign up to one club or society at the freshers' fair, and you should collect as many money off vouchers as you can – you never know when you'll use them.

You need to complete all the admin with your department this week. Don't forget to sign up with a doctor if your university doesn't have a medical centre.

Remember to consider your personal safety at all times by making sure you have a cab number and know the times and routes of the buses at night. You are in a location that is probably unfamiliar to you, so buy an A-Z or download Google Maps and plan how you will get to (and return from) destinations safely.

# Chapter Three
# Money Matters

'Money is always tight at university. I think the best way is just to have a budget for the week that you try and stick to. There is no point assigning how much money you're going to spend on a certain thing because you will never stick to it. But setting a weekly budget that is realistic is a good way of keeping on track. I have started writing down what money I spend, just so I know where it has gone at the end of the month, but that's not for everyone.' Jane.

This will probably be the first time in your life when you need to manage money. The best way of doing this is to draw up a budget so that you know exactly what you have to spend and where you may have to make economies.

## Tuition fees

Your parents may have agreed to pay your tuition fees, in which case they will have made an arrangement with the university. Many students take out a loan to pay their fees (see below) and this amount is paid directly to the university.

## Student loan

As part of your loan, your tuition fees will be paid straight to the university. The rest of your loan will be paid into your bank account each term (monthly if you go to a Scottish university).

Try to put a proportion of this money into an instant access (one that you can get money out of at any time) savings account so it will earn interest for you. Take a look at www.moneysupermarket.com or www.moneysavingexpert.com to find out which accounts will give you the best deals.

'Do not spend all of your student loan in one go – remember, most of it goes into paying for your accommodation!'
Libby.

Remember, you will have to repay your student loan once you have left university and are earning over £15,000 on a pro rata basis – the more you earn, the greater your monthly repayments. Therefore, it is in your own best interests to keep your overdraft to a minimum and to save as much money as you can from working during the holidays.

If you have any problems regarding your student loan, contact Student Finance Direct. Their contact details can be found in the help list, but you could also visit their website at www.direct.gov.uk/studentfinance for information. See the help list for further contact details.

## Bursaries

If your family income is less than £25,000, you will be entitled to a full bursary of £2906. There is a sliding scale for this, so that you would get £50 if your household income amounts to £60,000. Every little helps and this is an amount you won't have to pay back.

Both you and your parent(s) will have had to complete forms for this, giving proof of income, and you should have heard before you set off for university whether or not you've been awarded the bursary.

You may also find that your university gives grants to students on full bursaries, so check these out. This normally happens automatically via the university finance department. However, you may find that when they give you this money, the amount and when it's paid can vary. For example, at Manchester university students on a full bursary receive another £1000 but this is paid in three installments: £200 in December, £300 in January and £500 in March.

## Scholarships

You can check if you are eligible for any scholarships at www.scholarship-search.org.uk.

Your university may also make you an award if you have attained certain grades at A level. Again, this is money that you do not have to repay so it's well worth having.

## Parental contribution

If your parents are contributing to your expenses, they will have to pay your accommodation costs direct to the university's halls of residence. They will be offered various ways of paying in installments.

If they are also providing money for your living expenses, it's probably wise for them to make monthly payments into your bank account rather than termly ones. This will help you budget and will prevent you from spending all the money as soon as it's paid in!

## Overdrafts

If you can, try to leave your overdraft facility for emergencies. You may need to pay a deposit on your second year accommodation as early as the first term, which you probably won't have made a provision for.

# Overspending

If you find that you are spending more than you anticipated, take stock of what your outgoings are. If you have already prepared a budget, refer to it to work out where the extra money is being spent. It may be something simple like not taking into account how much your meals at university are costing or spending too much on socialising!

If you haven't set a budget, start thinking about one. A good way of monitoring your spending is to write down all that you spend each day, for a week. You may see a pattern emerging – one where you'll be able to make savings. For instance, you may have been buying a newspaper every day and this could amount to nearly £8. Multiply that up for the term and you'll see how much you could save by reading the newspapers in the library. Alternatively, you may have been buying too many ready meals or takeaways, so you would need to think about what you are eating and start to cook food yourself. See chapter 7 for more information on food and cooking.

'If you find that you are spending more than you anticipated, take stock of what your outgoings are. If you have already prepared a budget, refer to it to work out where the extra money is being spent.'

You can find information on planning a budget on most university websites. Basically, you need to write down all your outgoings per term (accommodation), per week (food, etc) and per day (drinks at uni, etc). You will also need to take into account travel expenses, books and toiletries.

Learning to budget and control your finances is a valuable lesson to be learned at university which will also help you once you are working.

# Earning money

Having a part-time job is the way many students cope with the expense of university. However, while it may be great to be able to work through the holidays, working during term time can seriously affect your studies and social time, leaving you feeling exhausted. It's useful to have the extra cash, but you must make sure it's not being counterproductive. It is generally recommended that 16 hours a week is the maximum time a student should be in paid employment.

If you need to earn money, think of jobs that offer you the highest hourly rate. Many universities offer students admin work for about £10 an hour (jobs are advertised in the student union) – higher than the minimum wage which is what you'll probably get for most jobs in retail and hospitality. Pub and restaurant work are good standbys, but you may have to work very late shifts and then get up early for lectures. That will just make you feel grim and less able to study. On the plus side, you may be given meals, and working in the university bar means you'll be able to see your friends while you're working.

Never skip lectures for a job; you are at university to study for a degree. Look for work that has flexible hours but also offers you other benefits. For instance, babysitting one evening a week may mean you get to be in a warm, comfortable house and have a meal or snack as well. Ask around if anyone knows of someone needing a babysitter and check notice boards and shop windows. Don't put adverts in shop windows yourself – you'll never know who's contacting you and you should never put yourself at risk. Rates depend on the area but should include the cost of a cab back to your hall afterwards.

Another good way of raising your income is to offer tutoring. If you play a musical instrument you can offer lessons, or you could coach in your university subject.

You could also consider selling things on eBay. Some students have made a good income from buying things at a low price and reselling them at a higher one.

If there's an art department near you, they may be looking for life models. This is usually relatively well paid (and sitting still won't exhaust you – you can plan your next essay in you head!).

# Tips for saving money

- Sign up for Martin Lewis' email alert for the latest deals. It could be a magazine with a good mascara on the cover, free coffee somewhere or some useful two for one deals. You can find his website in the help list.

- Check out www.vouchers.co.uk for all sorts of discounts and vouchers for anything from clothes to books and restaurants.

- Shop in places that offer student discounts. If the discount isn't advertised, just ask.

- Find out what nights are the cheapest at the local cinema. Some cinemas have cheaper tickets on a Monday or Tuesday, or on all performances before a certain time in the evening.

- Sign up to Student Beans at www.studentbeans.co.uk for exclusive student deals and offers.

- Find a local hairdresser or hairdressing college that has a model night/day/afternoon – you can get your hair cut for free.

- Charity shops are great – go to the one in the most affluent area you can find as you'll get the best cast offs.

- Learn to sew (or find someone who can!) so you can adapt clothes to your size and personalise to your taste.

- Girls – go to the cosmetic departments in big stores and have your make-up done or ask about skincare – you'll probably be given some samples to try.

# Summing Up

Learning to budget and manage your finances is an important part of your new life away from home. The most important thing is to take control and know exactly what you have coming in and what expenses you have going out.

You need to be creative in how you save money by looking for all the deals and discounts on offer to you. You will find no end of help for local discounts at your student union. You will need to plan travel home so that you get the cheapest deals on coaches and trains.

If you plan to work during term time, make sure you don't take on too much as your coursework will suffer – 16 hours of work a week should be your absolute maximum. Try to go for the fewest hours with the highest hourly rate!

The same applies for holiday jobs – you don't want to be working all the time. You'll need to catch up with friends and relax too.

# Chapter Four

# Accommodation

'Self-catering is much better if you are quite independent already. If you are lazy, go with catered.' Guy.

As mentioned earlier, you'll probably look at the room that's going to be home for the next three terms and wonder why you came. You need to make it your space as soon as you can so that it will feel more like home and less like a cell!

If you haven't brought a plant with you, get one. House plants can help reduce stress, aid concentration and encourage you to be positive.

You can't do much about the colour of the walls but you can disguise it. Posters can be expensive, so think of making a collage out of postcards and flyers. However, you may find that your student union holds regular poster sales!

If you are living in a self-catering hall, you'll need to allocate your cupboard in the kitchen.

One thing to remember is that it takes time to get to know new people, so don't make hasty judgements about your flatmates. However, if you are really unhappy with your accommodation for whatever reason, go to see your accommodation officer and ask about the possibility of changing halls. Most universities will be able to arrange this. You might also like to seek advice from the student union welfare officer.

'Learn how to use a washing machine!'

Joel.

## Living away from home

This will probably be the first time you have ever lived away from your parents. You are now responsible for all the things that seemed to get done miraculously at home – washing, cleaning, shopping for food, planning and preparing meals, entertaining and so on. Welcome to the real world!

If you are one of the lucky ones, your parents will have made sure that you know how to use a washing machine and can cook basic meals. Or maybe they tried to, but you weren't paying attention! Learning to live independently is often a steep curve, but you should have fun on the way.

## Sharing facilities – cleanliness and hygiene

Halls of residence tend to be cleaned, but don't expect too much. Your room will probably be your own responsibility and if you leave washing up in the kitchen sink, the cleaner won't do it for you. They are only there to provide a basic level of cleanliness in communal areas.

In some halls, individual rooms are cleaned, so make sure you know which day your cleaner is due. You don't want to get caught out in bed or having a shower!

'Invest in a pair of flip flops to wear in the bathroom and shower.'

Claire.

The more of you there are sharing accommodation, the more organised you have to be about clearing up and cleaning. (See the 10 commandments of flat sharing on page 39.)

## Sharing expenses

If you are living in catered accommodation, you don't have to worry about sharing expenses. However, during the first term in a non-catered hall it's a question of finding out what you want to share and individual tastes. You might like to have a kitty for buying tea, coffee and milk, but even this gets complicated if some people don't drink tea or coffee but use a lot of milk on their cereal. You all need to get together and decide what food you will share and what you will be buying separately.

Once you're in the second year and are house/flat sharing, you'll have to be far more organised. You must make sure that each person's name is on the lease and is responsible for paying their share of the rent and utility bills, like gas and electricity.

## Laundry

Remember the good old days when you just left your dirty washing on the floor of your room and it was returned to you clean and, if you were really lucky, ironed too?

Those days are over during term time and you need to get the hang of going to the launderette before you run out of clean clothes! To avoid having to separate light and dark colours, wash everything on a 30-degree wash cycle. Try to avoid overloading the machine as your clothes won't get cleaned properly, and turn them inside out to wash so any fluff picked up won't show on the right side.

If your clothes are stained, try treating them before washing by soaking in Oxiclean, which should do the job and doesn't contain any nasty chemicals. Less obstinate stains will respond to Oxiclean being added into the washing machine.

# Living at home

When I was at university in France, it was normal for students to go to their local university, which certainly wasn't the case in the UK at the time. However, because students now have to pay tuition fees and take out student loans rather than having grants, more UK students may end up studying closer to home and living with their parents.

There are, of course, other factors that come into the decision. Your local university may be the best place to study your chosen subject or you may have health considerations that make it more convenient to stay at home. Three students, Eliza, Lucy and Luke, give their reasons for studying in their home city.

'I chose to stay in London for a few reasons. The course I wanted to do was here and, in my opinion, London is the best place for art galleries and museums, which is essential for my course (women's wear, fashion design). Whether it is a conscious or subconscious decision, I guess it's always nice to stay somewhere you're familiar with, especially starting a new course. Perhaps I felt being somewhere else would be too much of a big move.

'I feel there are very few downsides to living in my home city as I love London! However, like any human being, you often feel like you need a change, which is something I feel every now and then, but then I remember how much I missed London when I was travelling!

'Another downside is that when starting a course, if it's in your home city it's unlikely that you'd move into halls as it would be cheaper to live at home, therefore you miss out a lot on the social aspects of university.' Eliza.

'I can't think of any reason why I wouldn't have stayed at home. Being frequently ill, it was important that there were people who could look after me from the start of university and, with a doctor on my road and my mum living with me, I had just that.

'On top of that, living at home is cheaper, easier and, given my home is in London, not in the middle of nowhere. I already have friends here and I know my way around, not to mention that my mum ensures I have a balanced diet with breakfast, lunch and dinner, and is always here to help.

'I suppose, however, I can see why one might want to move away. Freedom, individuality and the right to do exactly as you please all sounds very attractive. No longer bound by your parents' rules and regulations, you can go out every night and get home at any hour of the morning. To me, though, this wasn't much of an attraction because there's nothing I feel I can't do that I want to.

'I think that company is far more important to me than freedom, and I'm not sure I would have coped with university not having people who had known me for years to talk to about it every day of the week.' Lucy.

'Actually, I could have studied my subject in any number of places but I like living in London. I was really lucky to get a place in halls (Oxford Street!) which meant I really did have the best of both worlds. I had my independence in living away from home but could return at any time without having to pay huge fares and spend a lot of time travelling.' Luke.

# TV licence

It is your responsibility to make sure you are covered by a TV licence. Contrary to popular belief, you are not covered by your parents' licence. However, if you are living in halls, there is probably a licence to cover TVs in communal areas. Nevertheless, this will not cover you for watching TV in your room. If you are watching TV via a laptop, PC or mobile phone – in fact any device to receive television programmes – you must have a valid TV licence. If you are caught watching TV without a licence, you can be prosecuted and fined up to £1000.

If you are in a flat or house and have signed a joint tenancy agreement, you may only need one TV licence to cover all television receivers in the house. But if you have a separate tenancy agreement and you have a TV in your room, you'll need your own licence. This licence will also cover a TV in a communal sitting room.

If you buy your licence before the end of October and then return home for the summer holidays, you could qualify for a refund of up to £32. For more information on how to claim, call 0844 800 6779.

# Second year accommodation

At some point during your first year – maybe even during the first term – you will have to make a decision about who you would like to share with in the second year.

If you get on well with your current flatmates, that's a good starting point. However, if some of their habits are really getting on your nerves, then look to other friends you have made on your course or socially.

One very important point to remember is that you will be asked for a deposit to secure a flat or house for the following year. This can be as much as £500 to £600. You will have to find this money from somewhere and this may be the occasion to use your overdraft facility.

'At some point during your first year you will have to make a decision about who you would like to share with in the second year.'

When thinking about second year accommodation, check out your student union for any information packs to help you. You may also find that the housing officer will read through contracts for you and recommend landlords, but this isn't the case at every university. Ask any second or third year students you know to recommend landlords and visit their houses or flats to see the type of accommodation on offer.

You need to consider whether:

- It has a washing machine or is near to a launderette.
- It is near enough to university or a good bus service.
- It is in a safe area.
- Other students can recommend your landlord.

As a group, you may want to question the following:

- How long can you invite guests to stay?
- Is smoking permitted inside the house?
- How are bills going to be paid?
- Are you going to share food?
- Do you need a cleaning rota?

## *10 commandments for flat sharing*

- Leave the shower, bath and toilet as you would wish to find them – clean!

- Don't assume that toiletries left in the bathroom are for communal use.

- Make a decision about buying toilet rolls in bulk between you or getting your own. Always have your own supply in reserve, just in case.

- Empty the bin before it overflows (which isn't hygienic). The smell of old food is hardly appetising!

- Don't eat other people's food without asking.

- Respect other people's privacy.

- Don't go into someone else's room to borrow something if they are not there – it's their private space you're invading.

- Always knock before entering someone's room.

- Leave a post-it note on your door if you don't want to be disturbed.

- Don't make a noise coming home late at night – someone else could have an early start, important seminar or exam the next day.

## Summing Up

Where you are living can have a major impact on how you are feeling and how well you cope being away from home. If you have decided to stay at home, you may have to negotiate new rules!

Living in shared accommodation means you have to make allowances for other people as they do for you, but you should all agree on certain standards of hygiene and cleanliness. You also need to be considerate of other people with regards to noise and sharing bathrooms – all good experience for the future!

'Living in shared accommodation means you have to make allowances for other people as they do for you, but you should all agree on certain standards of hygiene and cleanliness.'

Your room may be your castle but make sure you remember to change your bed linen and take your clothes to the launderette. If you're trying to impress someone special, nothing is more off-putting than a dirty, smelly room!

# Chapter Five

# Sex and Relationships

Being at university can mean it's the first time you're living without parental supervision. No one to tell you what time to be in by or to check out who you are with and where you've been. It's a heady time. But it's also a time when you can suddenly feel a bit lost.

It may seem to you that everyone is having a great time sleeping around or finding a boyfriend or girlfriend. Maybe they are. But many students will be feeling uncertain. It takes time to develop a relationship and sex is only one facet of it.

If you consider every boy or girl you meet as a potential sexual partner – and therefore dismiss people out of hand – you will miss out on the opportunity of a wide and varied group of friends of both sexes.

Don't ever let someone pressurise you into having sex if you don't want to. Both males and females have a perfect right to say no.

> 'If you get a girlfriend at uni, be aware that all other girls seem to become hotter and more attracted to you. Strange.'
>
> Adrian.

## Gay, lesbian or bisexual?

At university you may discover (if you haven't done so already) that you don't fancy the opposite sex or that you are bi-sexual. Your student union will have information, helplines and support groups if you need them. The Stonewall website is a good place to start for information: www.stonewall.org.uk.

No one should ever tolerate or have to put up with homophobic behaviour. If you feel you are being discriminated against in any way, contact your student representative.

# Safe sex

Always practice safe sex. With the rise in STIs (see opposite) you should always be cautious. You will be given condoms during freshers' week and you can get free condoms from your GP. Make the most of this. If you have unprotected sex, you could be putting your health at risk. If you're a girl, you also stand a higher chance of getting pregnant.

## Emergency contraception

If a condom splits or you've had unprotected sex, seek out emergency contraception as soon as you possibly can.

'If a condom splits or you've had unprotected sex, seek out emergency contraception as soon as you possibly can.'

There are two options available to you if you do have unprotected sex. You can have an intra uterine device (IUD) fitted which stops a fertilised egg from embedding itself into the womb or you can take the morning after pill. If the pill is taken within 24 hours after sex, it will prevent 95 out of 100 pregnancies. At 72 hours after sex the success rate falls to 58%.

An IUD has to be fitted by a GP or nurse practitioner – phone to check that there is someone qualified to perform this at your surgery or go to a Brook Centre or genitourinary (GUM) clinic. Having the IUD fitted may feel a bit uncomfortable but it will also continue to work as a contraceptive. However, you should not rely on this unless you are in a long term partnership. Condoms should still be worn for protection against STIs.

The morning after pill is available free of charge from some pharmacies, GPs, Brook Centres, NHS walk-in centres and from most sexual health clinics. You will have to check this out via the local Primary Care Trust (PCT) website or your student union may have details. You can pay for the pill (about £24) if your chosen pharmacy isn't part of this scheme. Expect a short interview with the pharmacist. This is totally confidential but obligatory.

For more detailed information about the morning after pill, see *The Pill – An Essential Guide* (Need2Know).

# Sexually transmitted infections (STIs)

You don't have to be promiscuous to pick up an STI. You may have had sex with only one person, but if he or she is infected then you are likely to be as well. STIs are no joke and can have far reaching and long term effects on your health and future fertility. Two of the most common STIs are chlamydia and genital herpes.

## Chlamydia

Chlamydia is the most common treatable STI. Unfortunately, it has very few symptoms and therefore risks being undiagnosed. If you are sexually active and under 25, you have a one in 10 chance of having chlamydia. If you are under 20, your risk is even greater.

The National Chlamydia Screening Programme (NCSP) offers screening outside of GUM services. Both males and females under 25 can be tested as part of the programme. Go to www.chlamydiascreening.nhs.uk and enter your postcode to find your local free testing service.

Chlamydia can affect the fertility of both sexes but can be treated easily with antibiotics. If you are infected it is important that your partner is treated, as well as any previous partners. Repeated infection can worsen fertility problems in women.

## Genital herpes

Genital herpes is contagious and is primarily an STI. A cold sore can infect the genitals through oral sex and the virus is still contagious even when there are no visible blisters or ulcers.

If you suspect you have been infected, see your GP for a referral to a GUM clinic for diagnosis and the appropriate medication. The first bout is usually the worst and can leave you feeling really ill. Some people have few subsequent attacks but others have them regularly.

To avoid genital herpes, always use a condom and use one for oral sex as well.

# When relationships end

It doesn't matter who dumped who – it hurts! Even if you are the one to end a relationship, you might feel down afterwards. Although you may feel it is the end of the world, it isn't. However, people telling you that he or she wasn't good enough for you/you're well rid/there are plenty more fish in the sea, doesn't make it any easier to bear.

Remember that although you can't change how you feel, you can change how you think about it. Thinking positively can help you feel better.

If you need to talk to someone and would rather not talk to friends or family, contact a student counsellor or a helpline. A useful website to visit is www.nightline.niss.ac.uk. Your student union will also be able to suggest further sources of support.

'If you need to talk to someone and would rather not talk to friends or family, contact a student counsellor or a helpline.'

# Long distance relationships

If you and your boyfriend or girlfriend find yourselves at different ends of the country, it may seem almost impossible to keep a relationship alive. However, just like teen marriages and parenthood, sometimes it works and sometimes it doesn't.

Only you can be the judge of your relationship and what you want out of it. You should try not to miss out on all the socialising at university just because your other half isn't there. It isn't just a degree you are getting, but a whole experience.

There's a complete section on the NUS website devoted to long distance relationships, with a message board where you can share experiences, ask questions and seek advice from other students who are going though similar situations. Visit www.nus.org.uk to get chatting.

You could download Skype for free UK phone calls with the added benefit of being able to see each other on screen. To find out more visit www.skype.com.

# Family contact

Parents hope their children are having a marvellous time at university and making the most of all the opportunities available – as well as studying. They would, of course, also like to know you are still alive from time to time.

If your parents have signed up to a social networking site like Facebook (and you have too), they'll be able to keep track of your antics and see all the embarrassing photos and comments you have!

However, make sure you give them a call now and again just to let them know how you are feeling and to ask their news. Don't make this a regular call at a certain time every week – the first time you don't phone as usual, your parents will be imagining the worst!

A postcard or letter to other members of your family or close friends will also be appreciated.

# Summing Up

Relationships change when you move away from home. Some pass the test of time and distance and others don't. However, in the digital age there is no reason for not keeping in touch with friends and family.

Enjoy the freedom you have but always remember to practice safe sex. You might make a mistake and feel awful after a one night stand, but at least you won't have to deal with all the implications of an STI or an unwanted pregnancy.

If a condom splits, take advantage of emergency contraception as soon as possible. You may also want to be tested for chlamydia, one of the most prevalent STIs. For more information on STIs, read *Sexually Transmitted Infections – The Essential Guide* (Need2Know).

If you have questions about your sexuality, seek advice and never feel that you have to put up with homophobia or bullying.

# Chapter Six

# Health and Fitness

'Your uni should provide a questionnaire at the freshers' fair for you to fill in to register at a doctor's surgery. Do this. Even if you never get ill or hate visiting the doctor, it's better to be safe than sorry. If the uni do not supply this, ask.' Libby.

'This was easy for me because the university has a medical centre especially for this and a website with the registration form on. It's just a case of filling it in and sending it off. Make sure you do register because it's important to have somewhere to go if you are unwell which, unfortunately, happens to everyone.' Jane.

## Signing up with a GP and dentist

You should have signed up with a doctor/health clinic during freshers' week. However, if there's no medical centre at your university, you can check with your union for GPs who are willing to take on students.

The same applies for a dentist – but generally speaking you'll only need one if you need treatment as you will probably maintain your dentist at home. Some teaching hospitals have emergency dental clinics. Again, you should check this with your union.

## Prescription charges

Prescription charges were recently abolished in Wales and Scotland after successful campaigning by NUS Scotland and Wales. This year the NUS is lobbying the government to abolish prescription charges for students in the rest of the UK.

'You should have signed up with a doctor/ health clinic during freshers' week. However, if there's no medical centre at your university, you can check with your union for GPs who are willing to take on students.'

Students may qualify for an exemption to charges on the grounds of low income. However, you need to fill in an HC1 form when you start at university. Your student advice centre should have some, as will your GP and dentist. If you qualify, the HC1 certificate will help with many health costs and allow you to receive some of your prescriptions for free.

However, according to the NUS website, this current system of claiming through an HC1 form is costly, bureaucratic and may act as a deterrent to students accessing healthcare.

If your doctor gives you a prescription, check whether you can buy the medicine (or an equivalent) over the counter.

## Keeping fit

'It's cheaper to join your university gym for three years than to join a normal one for six months, so make the most of it!'

Joel.

Try to find at least one physical activity you like and make sure you do it. It's a good idea to sign up with one of the sports clubs during freshers' week as you are more likely to continue with something if it's a group activity right at your doorstep.

As an antidote to all that sitting and studying, aim to be as active as possible. Ideally, you should exercise for about 30 minutes, four or five times a week. Ordinary activities like walking to the shops and running up and down stairs instead of taking lifts all help to keep you fit and healthy.

If you find the thought of going to an exercise class off-putting, buy a DVD of an exercise you enjoy doing – there are so many to choose from. Exercising releases hormones called endorphins, which are mood enhancers.

Yoga is also an excellent way of keeping your body and mind fit. Join a class or buy a DVD. The breathing techniques learned in yoga help to aid relaxation and you can do most of them at any time to help wind down – on a bus, during an exam or before a presentation. Yoga also helps with concentration and motivation.

# Looking after yourself

You are now responsible for yourself and you need to make sure you eat properly, get enough exercise and take care of any problems as they arise.

Most infections like a cold or sore throat go away on their own – our bodies have amazing self-healing properties. However, you shouldn't leave some health matters to chance. If you are worried about something, consult a medical practitioner. Be wary of checking symptoms on the Internet as this may worry you further. Only use reliable sites like www.netdoctor.co.uk, www.sugerydoor.co.uk and www.nhs.uk.

# Feeling down or anxious

Moving home is rated by psychologists as one of the most stressful times in a person's life. Added to this, students are leaving friends and family, meeting new people and possibly worrying about money, living conditions, coursework and exams!

It's an explosive cocktail. But rest assured that any anxiety you may be feeling will not last forever. You are not alone and there are people out there to support you. Talking about your feelings will help put you back in control and to see the choices that are open to you. Things will begin to make sense again.

Most people (regardless of whether they are a student or not) feel anxious at times, so don't be embarrassed or afraid to seek help. Bottling up feelings will only make you feel worse. Talk to someone – friends, family, tutors or counsellors – and let them know how you're feeling. Your university will have a welfare office you can contact if you need help with problems associated with drugs, alcohol, eating disorders and depression. Visit your student union as your first port of call.

If you prefer to talk to someone who doesn't know you, there are various helplines available that will offer support and advice and, of course, you can remain anonymous.

'You are now responsible for yourself and you need to make sure you eat properly, get enough exercise and take care of any problems as they arise.'

## Students Against Depression

This website is an excellent place to start if you are feeling depressed or are worried about a friend who is showing signs of depression. There are sections on how depression works, putting it into context and self-help strategies for tackling the problem as well as getting help and support. It also has real life stories from students showing how depression can be overcome. Visit www. studentdepression.org to find out more.

## Nightline

Run by students for students, Nightline offers anonymous and confidential support and information. Visit the website to find your local service: www. nightline.ac.uk.

## Samaritans

Samaritans is a registered charity offering a 24-hour service for emotional support. The helpline number is 08457 909090.

## Volunteer

While at university you could volunteer to help a charity or organisation. By helping others you can put your own experiences into perspective. It's also a good way to gain experiences for future careers. Visit www.timebank.org.uk or www.do-it.org to find out more.

## Eating disorders

Feeling anxious or stressed out can affect the way you view yourself. Sometimes people who feel out of control in one way like to control what they eat. In extreme cases, this can lead to anorexia or bulimia. If you think you have a problem with an eating disorder, try this website for help and support: www.b-eat.co.uk.

## Illegal drugs

If you think have a problem with illegal drugs or would like to know more, go to www.talktofrank.com.

## Alcohol

Your liver is an amazing organ but it can only suffer so much abuse. Overindulgence in alcohol will make you feel tired, depressed, irritable and generally out of sorts – not to mention hard up!

There's no cure for a hangover (if there was, someone would be very rich!), but you can aim to minimise the effects:

- Try to drink juice or water between each alcoholic drink.

- Never drink on an empty stomach – the alcohol will go straight to your head. Eat slow release carbohydrates like pasta before drinking.

- Don't mix your drinks – this adds to the number of toxins in your body.

- Light coloured drinks (white wine, gin and vodka) contain fewer impurities.

- Drink a couple of glasses of water before going to bed and have some ready in case you wake up during the night.

If you think you have a problem with alcohol or you would like some advice and support, contact Drinkline on 0800 917 8282. You can also learn more about your drinking habits at www.drinkcheck.nhs.uk.

'Overindulgence in alcohol will make you feel tired, depressed, irritable and generally out of sorts – not to mention hard up!'

# Top health tips

- If you are continually overindulging in alcohol, your liver will suffer. Try to have at least two days a week alcohol-free.

- Don't binge drink at weekends – or any time!

- Five portions of fruit and vegetables a day is the minimum to aim for. A glass of juice counts as one portion. Potatoes do not count as a vegetable, but you could eat them with their skins on for a good source of vitamin C (and it will save time on peeling!).

- Exercise as much as you can as the endorphins released by exercise will make you feel better mentally and physically. Dancing counts, as does going for a brisk walk. Aim to exercise at least three times a week but incorporating some physical activity into each day (walking to uni, etc) will have beneficial effects.

- Make sure you drink plenty of fluids. If you feel thirsty it means you are already dehydrated and will find it much harder to concentrate.

- Don't smoke. Smoking is one of the worst things you can do for your health and you won't be able to afford it. It's just burning money.

- Wear a sunscreen. On the aesthetic front, your skin will show wrinkles and fine lines much earlier if constantly exposed to the sun. Incidence of skin cancer in the UK is doubling every 10 years – be warned.

# Summing Up

Your health is your most important asset. Keep yourself physically fit and you will benefit mentally. You need to look after both your body and your mind.

Make sure you have signed up with a GP or the university medical centre (and have their number listed on your mobile phone) as you never know when you may need medical help. You will also need a doctor's certificate if you are ill and cannot complete an assignment or attend an exam.

If you are feeling depressed, have problems with alcohol or drugs or worry you may be developing an eating disorder, please seek advice. You do not have to cope alone. The earlier you find help, the better.

Following the top health tips in this chapter should help you keep on form.

'Your health is your most important asset. Keep yourself physically fit and you will benefit mentally.'

# Chapter Seven
# Food

'Suggest to your flatmates that you should all have a weekly meal together, sharing the cost and responsibilities (if you can't cook – offer to wash up!). Alternatively, you could offer to do a food share where you cook in pairs or threes, each taking a turn.' Libby.

The quality of the food you eat makes an enormous difference to how you feel physically and mentally. It's a bit of a shock when you have been used to home cooked meals to discover that you can't afford the same sort of food or don't know how to make it. It can be quite a disappointment if you don't like the food served in your catered halls either.

'The quality of the food you eat makes an enormous difference to how you feel physically and mentally.'

## Catered halls

'I think it depends on the university, but here in Nottingham the catered halls are really popular because of their location. It is a campus university and so they are all very near to the lecture halls/library, while all the self-catered accommodation is a fair walk off campus.

'A definite advantage of being in catered halls is that although it is a bit like boarding school (all being in long corridors and eating every meal together), it is very sociable. There are 300 people in my hall and I recognise or know most of them. We have a bar and a common room where everyone hangs out.

'Obviously we can be quite lazy as we don't need to go on weekly food shops or wash up after ourselves; we merely scrape our plate and put it in a pile, so it is very easy. At Nottingham there is a really good system whereby catered students have a meal card which has £4.50 on it for lunch and we can use it in any cafe or food outlet across the campus. For the average person £4.50 is ample, so we normally buy loads of extra food just to get our money's worth!

'I have a lot of early lectures so I normally get up for breakfast which finishes at 9.30, but quite a few of my friends don't. We worked out that we are theoretically spending about £500 on breakfast for the whole year, which seems ridiculous when you think how often people miss it!

'All the girls complain because they eat too much and blame it on being catered. I know that a lot of people are claiming they have put on weight when all my self-catered friends hardly eat because they can't be bothered. Even if you're not hungry, you go to lunch or dinner anyway because you have paid for it and you want to get your money's worth. We get soup and bread, a main course and then a dessert every dinner-time.

'Loads of boys spend a lot of money on takeaways because we all go to dinner at 5.30 when it starts, so by the time it's 10.30 you're hungry again! Sometimes there are really horrible food options and you are left disappointed. But it is quite exciting going to dinner every day and wondering what will be on offer!

'I think it differs from university to university, but I figured I have got my whole life to cook for myself so I might as well be lazy for my first year of university!' Tash.

'I was in catered halls at Cambridge but as I was studying music, most of my rehearsal times clashed with the evening meal. There was nothing anybody would do about this so it was a complete waste of money and I had to find places to eat out.' Ellen.

> 'When you plan a meal, think about the colours of the food. The more colours there are on your plate, the more nutritious your meal.'

## Self-catering

'Try to find three or four dishes that you can cook before going to university – there is nothing more depressing than returning from a day of lectures to find your flatmates all eating home cooked food and you have to eat toast!' Libby.

While it's very tempting to buy ready-made meals, they are often expensive and full of additives and extra salt, sugar and fats that our bodies can do without. If 'you are what you eat' then you really should go for the best food you can afford. However, try to remember that the best doesn't always mean the most expensive.

Always go for wholemeal bread and pasta and wholegrain rice as they are far more nutritious than the alternatives. When you plan a meal, think about the colours of the food. The more colours there are on your plate, the more nutritious your meal.

Don't be conned into buying so-called 'superfoods' – this is just an advertising term and these foods are more than likely going to be very expensive. Eat a varied diet and remember that some foods, like carrots, have more goodness in them when eaten raw.

If you need some recipes, consult *Student Cookbook – Healthy Eating – The Essential Guide* (Need2Know). For an in-depth look at nutrients and how they act together – in a good or bad way – read Ian Marber's *Supereating* (Quadrille).

# Eating out

When you're having meals on campus, try to choose things that you don't make in your flat and avoid the foods (and you know what they are!) that are unhealthy options. But remember to give yourself a treat now and then!

If there is a FE college nearby, see if they have a subsidised restaurant which is run by trainee chefs – good food and lower prices!

Take advantage of all the two for one offers that are available in restaurants. Check out www.myvouchers.co.uk and www.moneysupermarket.com to get the best deals.

# Storing food

Some foods need to be kept in the fridge to help stop bacteria from growing on them, such as those with a use-by date, cooked foods and ready-to-eat items like desserts and cooked meats.

## Sharing a fridge

While it might seem sensible to each have a shelf (or half a shelf!) in the fridge, this is not a good way of storing foods. There is a definite hierarchy in a fridge!

On the top shelf you should have dairy products. Fruit and vegetables go in the salad compartments. Cooked meats should go above and be separate from uncooked meats and poultry, which should be in clean, sealed containers on the bottom shelf of the fridge so they can't touch or drip onto other food.

## Food poisoning

'Always thoroughly clean plates, utensils and surfaces after they have touched raw or thawing meat to stop bacteria from spreading. And, it goes without saying, always be sure to wash your hands.'

According to the Food Standards Agency, an estimated 5.5 million people in the UK are affected by food poisoning each year. Only a small number of these visit their GP or get medical advice. Most people recover from the symptoms of sickness and diarrhoea within a day or so, but prevention is better than cure and you certainly don't want to risk an attack of food poisoning before an important seminar, exam or social event!

Many foods don't need to be kept in the fridge to keep them safe to eat. Dry foods such as rice, pasta and flour, many types of drinks, tinned foods and unopened jars can all be kept elsewhere. But it's still important to take care when storing these foods.

Always thoroughly clean plates, utensils and surfaces after they have touched raw or thawing meat to stop bacteria from spreading. And, it goes without saying, always be sure to wash your hands.

## Storing food safely:

- Keep food fresh in sealed bags or containers. This will stop anything (including unwanted visitors like mice and insects) falling into the food by accident.

- Don't store food on the floor because this can entice mice, ants and other pests.

- Keep the storage areas dry and not too warm – don't put anything next to a heater or cooker!

- Remember that some foods have to be kept in the fridge once they are opened (follow any storage instructions on the label) and probably have to be eaten within a day or two.

# Reducing waste

Throwing away food means you are wasting money, so you need to plan what you want to eat and buy appropriately. Try not to cook more than you can eat (unless you are going to freeze it for another time – often cooking in big batches can save money and time) as you may not want to eat the same meal two days in a row!

## Use-by date

A lot of food gets wasted because it gets forgotten about at the back of the fridge and has passed its use-by date. Don't be tempted to consume any food or drink after the end of the use-by date on the label, even if it looks and smells fine. You could put your health at risk – see the previous section on food poisoning.

## Best before date

Best before dates are, as they suggest, more about quality than safety, so it doesn't mean that the food will have gone off when the date runs out. However, it might begin to lose its flavour and texture. Eggs are the exception to the rule – don't eat them after the best before date.

## Tin cans

If you are not going to use a whole tin of something straightaway, empty the remainder into a bowl or suitable container and put it in the fridge. You should never keep food in an opened tin can or re-use empty cans to cook or store food. When a can has been opened and the food is in contact with the air, the tin may transfer more quickly to the can's contents.

This advice doesn't apply to foods sold in cans with lids designed to reseal, such as golden syrup and cocoa.

## Cling film

Cling film is great for protecting food but needs to be used correctly.

Always check the packaging description to see what foods your cling film can be used with.

There are three main points to remember when using cling film:

- Don't use cling film if it could melt into the food, such as in the oven or on pots and pans on the hob.
- When using cling film in the microwave, make sure it doesn't touch the food.
- Only let cling film touch high-fat foods (some types of cheese, raw meats with a layer of fat, fried meats, pies, pastries and cakes with butter icing or chocolate coatings) when the packaging says it is okay to do so.

## Kitchen foil

Kitchen foil made from aluminium can be useful for wrapping and covering foods. But it's best not to use foil or containers made from aluminium to store foods that are highly acidic, such as tomatoes, rhubarb, cabbage and soft fruits. This is because aluminium can affect the taste of these sorts of food, especially if they are stored in aluminium containers for a long time.

# Money saving tips

- Sign up for a loyalty card where you shop regularly. Boots and Sainsbury's will give you money off and Tesco sends you money off vouchers. These are worth four times as much if you trade them in for air miles, days out or restaurant vouchers. All three send you coupons to earn more points on your shopping.

- Buy one get one free offers are not particularly useful for produce that has a short life span but to take advantage of them, go shopping with a friend and share offers.

- Sometimes buying in larger quantities does not make sense – you may find a bigger jar of coffee is more expensive than two smaller ones. It pays to check prices compared to amounts carefully. A few extra minutes can save you pounds!

- Make your own muesli using supermarket own brand oats and adding the dried (or fresh) fruits and nuts you like.

- Supermarket own brands or value brands are cheaper and often just as good as proprietary brands (often made by the same companies!).

- Buy frozen vegetables – they are frozen when picked so are often fresher than any others you can buy, plus you can cook the exact amount you want without wastage.

- Certain canned beans, tomatoes and vegetables are an excellent standby to have in the cupboards and can make really tasty meals!

- Keep a supply of dried pasta and rice – the basis for so many meals.

- Don't buy large bags of fruit and vegetables which may go off before you have the chance to eat them. It may seem more expensive to buy two carrots but it's more cost-effective than throwing away half a bag.

- Buy hard fruits like apples as they last longer than soft ones.

- Buy fruit and vegetables that are in season – they are less expensive and will help cut your carbon footprint!

'Poundland is often a false economy but Lidl is brilliant!'

Guy.

## Summing Up

If you are living in catered halls, try not to miss out on the meals you have already paid for. If you are fending for yourself, follow the tips and suggestions in this chapter for eating healthily as well as economically.

How you store and prepare food can have a major impact on its nutritional value. Look after your food properly so you don't have to waste any. Throwing away food is like throwing away your money!

Don't rely on takeaways and ready prepared meals which have little nutritional value and, even if cheap, are not cost effective if all they are doing is filling you up without nourishing you. If you haven't learned how to cook yet, think about making simple meals that make the most of produce in season.

'How you store and prepare food can have a major impact on its nutritional value. Look after your food properly so you don't have to waste any.'

# Chapter Eight

## Getting to Know Your Department

'Try not to study when all your flatmates are in or on nights when you all usually go out. This will only distract you and make you less likely to get anything done. Instead, try going to the library or studying in groups, where you will feel more relaxed and inclined to work.' Libby.

During freshers' week you'll find out where your department is. Make sure you go to any induction lectures – give yourself plenty of time to get to them in case you get lost. Have a good look around the building and familiarise yourself with the layout for lecture halls, seminar rooms and the toilets!

Knowing where to go for your first lecture means you'll have one less thing to worry about. Being prepared takes some of the stress out of new situations.

If a tour is offered, go on it so you are sure you know exactly what is available and where to find it.

**'You can usually change units or modules quite easily, so don't get stuck with something if you hate it.'**

Joel.

## Timetables

Your first term timetable will probably be on the university website, but remember you may have to add in special subjects and options. Print yourself a copy of your timetable and have it handy at all times.

If you have any queries about your timetable, think you may have a subject clash or can't find a room, ask your department office for help. They'll be able to answer all your questions and are used to students asking for help.

## Special subjects and options

There may be some core subjects that you are required to take in your first year and, therefore, you won't get a choice.

However, you may also have some extra subjects to choose from. Don't delay – make an appointment to see your tutor (see below) and discuss what is on offer as soon as possible. You'll probably find that some options are non-starters because they clash with other things on your timetable, so go with an open mind. If you leave it too late you won't have much to choose from as classes will be full.

'In my first term I saw my personal tutor once. When I tried to make an appointment with her, she told me she wouldn't be available!'

Zoe.

# Personal tutors

Personal tutors are members of the department to whom each student is allocated. How much contact time you actually have with a personal tutor varies, so don't expect to be able to see him or her at a whim. You'll need to make an appointment.

Unlike school, you don't have automatic access to the academic staff. However, you should be able to contact your lecturers and tutors by email. This may be the best way of contacting them if you have general questions that can be sorted out easily.

However, if you have a problem and are unable to see your tutor for whatever reason, contact your course student representative (see overleaf) and ask him or her who you should contact. You don't have to discuss the problem but you should be given the name of someone you can speak to.

# Peer group

When you were at school, in the sixth form or at college, the chances are you were probably one of the best and brightest students. Once you get to university, it may come as a shock (and a bit of a blow to your ego) to find that some students are more able and confident than you are!

This is perfectly normal and it may just mean that some of the students exude more confidence. Don't lose heart – just as some babies walk and talk months before others, some students take longer to attune to their course.

'I was rather a mediocre student but somehow I always thought I could have done better. Then, in my final year, it all fell into place. My work and understanding of my subjects improved. And I felt so much more confident about expressing my views.' Jenni.

## Course representatives

At the beginning of each academic year, course representatives are elected. These are the people you should contact for information or if you have a problem or suggestion.

Course representatives attend meetings with academic tutors where they share any student concerns or opinions. They also get the chance to give feedback to the Union Council.

This is something you should consider if you're interested in representation. You don't have to have experience, just the wellbeing of your co-students at heart, and training is provided. You get support from full time student officers, access to your tutors and the opportunity to improve your relationship with them. Being a course representative also looks great on your CV.

If you don't want to be involved at this level, make sure you know who your representative is – you never know when you may need to contact them.

## Students in other years

Get to know students in other years as they are an invaluable source of information! They can help when it comes to buying the best books and can assist you on your course. They will also be able to tip you off about the best landlords and areas to live after your first year.

# Help - I've made a mistake!

What happens if you realise that the course you're studying isn't for you? Maybe it's not what you expected or the subject is being taught in a way you don't feel comfortable with. Maybe you don't like the university or the area.

In the first instance you should make an appointment to see your personal tutor to find out if there is an element of your course you could change or receive help with. You could be referred to a careers advisor if you are unsure of what you really want to do. If you don't wish to talk about this with your personal tutor, arrange to see someone in student support. Your student union or course representative should be able to help you with this.

However, you may have decided that you really don't want to continue with the course you are on. According to Hannah Hunter, student support officer at the University of Cardiff, it would depend on the point in the academic year as to what you could do about it.

**'Get to know students in other years as they are an invaluable source of information!'**

If it is in the first couple of weeks it may be possible for you to transfer immediately, so you should contact the relevant admissions tutor for the course you'd like to transfer to and to find out if there are any places available. If a place is available and you have the correct entry requirements, it may be possible to change immediately.

If you decide later in the term that you want to leave, it's unlikely that you would be able to transfer. In this case you would have to find out from the admissions tutor if you would be offered an unconditional place for the next academic year or if you need to reapply through UCAS.

Find out from your union or course representative who you have to contact in the university administration department to make sure you complete all the relevant admin, including giving up your room in halls and returning the key. You will be charged hall fees until the date the key is returned. You will also be required to return your student card.

You will have to contact the Student Loans Company and Local Education Authority (LEA) if you are receiving a bursary. Any maintenance loan you received would fall under the normal terms and condition of the loan and will not be required to be repaid immediately.

The main thing is that you seek advice from your university so that you follow all the necessary procedures.

## Summing Up

Studying at university is so different from your school days that it may take you some time to get the hang of it all. Take advantage of all the help there is, especially from students in the second and third years who should be able to put you straight on many issues. Remember you have course representatives who can find things out for you or forward any suggestions you have at meetings.

Give yourself time to settle in before deciding that you may have made the wrong choice – either of course or university. If you do have real concerns about where you are and what you are studying, don't keep them to yourself and don't just pack up and go home. Seek advice from the appropriate student support officers.

'Studying at university is so different from your school days that it may take you some time to get the hang of it all.'

# Chapter Nine
## Studying and Assessed Work

'Assessed work is always something students leave to the last minute – I speak from experience. Try to make a plan beforehand, even if you still leave it late – this will help you become less stressed and provide you with the framework for the essay or work.' Libby.

One of the first things you have to get to grips with at university is the amount of free time you have. You'll notice when you start your course how few lectures, seminars and tutorials you have compared to when you were at school.

Subjects vary in the amount of contact time you have with your lecturers. Don't be fooled into thinking this is a breeze – you read for a degree at university and most of your time will be spent studying your text books, reading around the subject and researching for essays and any presentations you may have to give, as well as doing practicals. This all takes time, so having two days when you don't attend any lectures isn't an invitation to stay in bed all day or go off on a jaunt.

You may find it helpful to make a weekly timetable so that you can arrange your time productively. Apart from your lectures, seminars and tutorials, include study time, sporting activities, socialising and shopping so each day has a structure.

'You may find it helpful to make a weekly timetable so that you can arrange your time productively.'

# Assessed work

- Make sure you understand exactly what is required. If you don't – ask!

- Follow the format you have been asked to submit, especially regarding footnotes and referencing. This may take you a while to get the hang of but it's an important part of your learning curve (in some subjects you can lose marks for not presenting work in the right style).

- Don't plagiarise. Don't copy an essay you've found on the Internet or pass something off as your own that has been copied from a text book or website. If you want to quote someone, make sure you follow the referencing rules for your course. Plagiarism is taken seriously at university – it could result in you losing your place on your course.

- Before you hand in your work, read it through carefully (print out a copy, don't do this on screen) and make sure you have fulfilled all the criteria. Do not rely on spell-checks on your computer – use a dictionary to check words you are unsure of.

- Keep to deadlines – you won't be able to ask your mum or dad to send in a note for you. If you have a genuine reason for seeking an extension, see your tutor in plenty of time, not the day before an essay is due. If you are ill, you'll need a doctor's certificate.

## Making drafts

One of the best ways of planning an essay or piece of work is to use what is known as a Mind Map (patented by Tony Buzan). On a clean sheet of paper, start off with the title in the centre. Using different colours, draw curvy lines out for each main point and then little lines branching off for supporting ideas. This will help you think laterally and creatively. This is also an excellent tool for revision. Visit www.buzanworld.com for more information.

# Recommended reading

If you don't want to end up buying all the recommended books, make sure you get to the library as soon as you can to borrow them. Alternatively, check out the second-hand bookshops or see if you can borrow them from a student in a different year group.

## Libraries

Make use of your libraries and be on friendly terms with librarians, who are an invaluable source of information and advice. They should be numbered amongst your new best friends!

Return your books on time – library fines are just a waste of your precious and limited money!

# Create the right conditions for studying

- You may find you work well in your room or that there are too many distractions and are better off in a library.

- Make sure you're warm and comfortable.

- Have everything you need to hand so you don't have to keep stopping to search for things.

- Clear any clutter. It makes life so much easier when you can see and find things straightaway!

- We have got used to living in a 24/7 culture but you have to learn to focus your attention. Switch off your mobile phone and the Internet. You can check for messages when you take a break.

'Make use of your libraries and be on friendly terms with librarians, who are an invaluable source of information and advice. They should be numbered amongst your new best friends!'

## Study techniques

You may already have found good ways of studying that worked for you while you were taking your A levels or diplomas. There is never one right way to study but, generally speaking, the more proactive you are (taking notes, creating diagrams and making prompt cards), the more effective your studying will be.

# Summing Up

If you haven't done so already at school, you will have to find the study techniques that suit you best. Some people find working in libraries to be most beneficial while others prefer the seclusion of their own room. Whatever works for you, you will no doubt benefit from a change of scene from time to time.

Make sure you plan your workload so that you meet deadlines – always allow more time than you think you'll need just in case of any hitches.

Time that is not scheduled for lectures and seminars is time for you to study, read and prepare your work, not to waste sleeping in! On the other hand, time used creatively and productively for sport or physical activity or helping out in a volunteer capacity will have knock on benefits when you go back to your studying.

'If you haven't done so already at school, you will have to find the study techniques that suit you best.

# Chapter Ten

# Exams

'Don't use re-takes as a back up plan because they ruin your summer. I know people who've had to cut short family holidays to come back for re-take exams, and the uni is really strict about it. You can't change the re-take dates at all. Don't plan to scrape 40% in your first year. You need (some of) what you learn for the rest of the course!' Joel.

## Planning your workload

Examinations are not designed to be a test of memory but of learning. You have to show the examiners that you have thought about your subject and have developed a well reasoned argument. They don't want you to regurgitate course notes or facts from text books. Your revision should be a consolidation of what you have been learning, not just cramming information.

Some students seem supremely confident about revising and sitting exams. They are in the minority – most of us get nervous just thinking about them! However, you can learn to prepare yourself so that you do the best you can.

Top athletes often say that on the days they feel under par, they push themselves the most. The theory is that if they do well then, they'll do even better when they are in peak condition. If you aim for this, you won't go far wrong. It's like taking a music exam and focusing your pieces until you can play them in your sleep – if you're overcome by nerves during the exam, your memory will take over.

'Start revising before you start to get anxious about it. If it is over Christmas, leave it until the New Year – give yourself time to relax.'

Zoe.

# Revision plan

The top tip for successful revision is to make a plan, otherwise it is easy to waste your precious time. It is helpful to look at your exam dates and work backwards to the first date you intend to start revising. Creating a revision plan will help you feel in control of the process.

Draw up a revision plan for each week, making sure you add in any regular activities you do. Please don't give up on all other activities as you need some fun time as well. Write up your plan and display it somewhere visible. However, try to be flexible – you may find you need more time on some subjects and less on others. It's best to start off with what you have the most trouble with so you have time to ask other students or your tutor if you need help.

Look at past papers from your department. You'll usually find these on your university website or in the library. Don't just read them, use them proactively. For example, try answering essay questions under exam conditions and time yourself. Alternatively, take each essay question and use it as a revision tool – write bullet points of what you would include in the answer.

## Tips for revision

- Plan to work for 50 minutes, then take 10 minutes to have a drink and a snack to keep you going. Stretching and breathing exercises are also useful when you're taking a break.

- Change what you are doing to keep you fresh. You could alternate topics or the way you are studying.

- Don't turn revision into a competition – other students won't necessarily tell the truth. Some will say they haven't done any revision and you can bet your life on the fact that they have. Alternatively, don't get competitive with your own revision.

- Have a change of venue – if you're feeling stressed, fed up or overloaded, take a walk to the library or your department for a change of scenery.

## Last-minute revision tips

Although time may be at a premium, you can still make a difference to your grade if you prioritise and do what you can.

- Don't panic – keep focused and think positively!

- Have confidence in yourself and think of what you have already achieved.

- Remember how you felt about exams in the past – did worrying about them make any difference to the outcome?

- Use your revision tools (prompt cards, diagrams, lists, etc) to have a final check of key facts, figures and so on.

- Try to keep calm and build on your existing knowledge rather than trying to learn new topics.

- Don't stay up all night revising. Being overtired will not help you to do your best.

# How to deal with exam nerves

It is natural to feel nervous before an examination. However, the more prepared you feel, the easier it will be to conquer your fears.

Plan your work carefully around the topics you need to devote more time to. Being aware of gaps in your knowledge may make you feel nervous, but having a plan of how you will fill these will make you feel better and more in control.

Allow yourself some time each day to relax – exercise is particularly good as a stress reliever.

Eat and drink sensibly – your brain cells need energy to function well. Make sure you drink plenty of water to avoid becoming dehydrated. Dehydration makes you tired and reduces concentration. Avoid caffeinated drinks.

If you're having problems sleeping, try to do something to wind down at the end of an evening studying. Relaxing baths, listening to music or watching a TV programme or DVD will help. Avoid alcohol as this is a depressant. Try green or herbal teas if you don't fancy a hot, milky drink.

Some people find taking Rescue Remedy or homeopathic remedies like Gelsemium and Aconite to be very useful for exam nerves.

'It is natural to feel nervous before an examination. However, the more prepared you feel, the easier it will be to conquer your fears.'

## Keeping focused

If you are feeling overwhelmed by everything you have to do, your stress levels will rise, making it so much harder for you to concentrate.

In her book *Find Your Focus Zone* (Simon & Schuster Ltd), Lucy Jo Palladino describes a four corner breathing exercise which you can do any time and anywhere to calm yourself quickly and regain your focus and concentration.

Look up from whatever you are doing and find something that has four corners – a picture, a door or the window below.

- Look at the upper left hand corner and inhale for the count of four.

- Move your gaze to the upper right hand corner and hold your breath for the count of four.

- Move your gaze to the lower right hand corner and exhale for the count of four.

- Move your gaze to the lower left hand corner, silently say the words, 'Relax, relax, smile' and do just that!

Breathe in...2,3,4          Hold... 2,3,4

'Relax, relax, smile'     Breathe out 2,3,4

# Sitting the exam

- Organise what you'll need to take with you (pens, pencils, ruler, scientific calculator, etc) the evening before.

- Be prepared. Find out what is involved in each of the examinations you are going to sit, where and when it will take place, how much time is allowed and how many questions you need to answer.

- Get a good night's sleep the day before.

- Eat a decent breakfast – you don't want to be hungry mid-exam!

- Leave for the exam in plenty of time.

- Have a watch so you can time yourself.

- Read the paper carefully to make sure you have understood the instructions and the questions.

- Choose questions that will show what you know to your best advantage.

- Don't spend too long on one question – if you answer only four out of five questions, you have already lost 20% of the marks.

- Be as neat as possible. Having to read virtually illegible scripts does not endear you to the person marking your paper.

- For essay questions, take a few minutes to write down the points you wish to cover – make sure you cross them out afterwards.

- Make sure you have 10 minutes at the end of the exam to read through your paper and correct any mistakes.

- If there is anything you don't wish the examiner to consider, cross it out.

# After the exam

Don't start worrying about how well you've done or discussing it with your friends on the course. Put this exam out of your mind and concentrate on the next one. There'll be enough time for post-mortems after the results!

Give yourself some time off and a bit of a treat before you start revising again. Make sure you get some exercise and a good meal.

Don't check your answers in your notes or text books – it's a waste of effort at this stage.

Think positively about what you have done and use each exam as a learning experience – is there anything you could have done differently in your revision or study plan? Use the revision styles below to find out which kind of studying suits you best. You could even alternate between the different styles next time you go to revise.

If your results are poor, see your tutor and get support and advice. Learn from the experience. Keep the exam in context – even if you do badly, there will be other options open to you.

# What sort of revision suits you best?

Think about how you learn or remember things:

■ Do you see them (visual)? Study by creating diagrams, ideas maps and colour coding.

■ Do you hear/talk about them (verbal/auditory)? Record summaries and listen to them. Revise by talking to people, explaining ideas and so forth.

■ Do you do them (active)? Engage with your revision material by taking notes and tap a rhythm to remember information by. Create sheets to fill in.

■ Do you think about them (reflective)? Stop and review what you are doing, write summaries and think about possible questions. Give yourself time to think about your ideas and what you are learning.

- Do you learn creatively (intuitive)? You dislike repetition and work which involves a lot of memorisation and routine calculations, so create your own tables, summaries and practice questions.

- Do you like facts and concrete examples (sensing)? Link information to the real world and revise by substituting different examples.

- Do you learn in detail and stepwise (sequential)? You like working methodically, step-by-step, building on detailed facts. Try to fill in sheets as well.

- Do you like the big picture first (global)? You could benefit from using concept maps, diagrams and flow charts.

Adapted from a flyer from Learning Skills Unit, University of Melbourne.

## Summing Up

Not many people enjoy exams but they have to be done. If you plan your revision well and pace yourself, you'll be okay. The important thing is to keep yourself focused and on target.

Your revision should be as proactive as possible – writing things down (however many times) sets them in your mind much more than just reading them.

Make sure you have everything you need for your exam in advance and try to have a good night's sleep before the big day. Once you have sat the exam, put it to the back of your mind and concentrate on the next. Wait for the results before you conduct the post-mortem!

'Your revision should be as proactive as possible – writing things down (however many times) sets them in your mind much more that just reading them.'

# Chapter Eleven

## Looking Forward

'Collect as many club positions as you can, especially in the first and second year. Basically, look for CV filler roles which sound good and you can talk about but in fact entail very little work.' Guy.

'Get on a committee to represent your faculty, department or student union. In reality, it's barely one meeting a term – looks good on your CV though.' Adrian.

'Think extra curricular activities – they are important to show balanced experience beyond that which is academic.' Joe.

'Do some volunteering – it will usually be free of any cost through the student union. It will be the easiest time to do it since you have loads of spare time. Usually there will be a huge range of choices and it will all be sorted for you. It looks great on your CV, you get to meet loads of nice people, you can escape the university bubble and do a nice thing in the process.' Guy.

'Go to recruitment evenings, fairs and events to get free food and drink plus goodies. I got a camera once!'
Jenna.

Going to university isn't just about getting a degree in a specific subject, it's acquiring knowledge and experience in the widest possible sense.

Once you have your degree and are looking for a job, your CV will need to stand out to get you even considered for a shortlist of candidates. Employers are looking for staff who can operate within a team as well as show creative and lateral thinking.

Your academic studies are just the beginning. While at university you need to accumulate as many 'brownie points' as you can. These will not only make you more attractive to potential employers but will also enrich your own experience of life as a student. Most of us only get one shot at being a student – so make the most of it!

# Plan your work experience

When looking for a job either during term time or the holidays, try to find something that will enhance your employability. If you plan to teach, try for a placement on a holiday play scheme or, during term time, an after-school club. If you think your career lies in the health sector, get a job in a hospital. It doesn't matter how lowly the job, what does matter is that you are gaining an appreciation of what happens in that environment. Make every job you take an asset to your CV.

# Volunteer

'Volunteering can bring you into contact with all kinds of professionals and people from every walk of life.'

Guy, in the quote over the page, comments on volunteering. However, one of the positive benefits he doesn't mention is how it will affect you personally. Being altruistic and helping other people has a powerful effect on the person volunteering. This is your chance to make a real difference to someone else's life and improve your own wellbeing along the way.

Volunteering can bring you into contact with all kinds of professionals and people from every walk of life. In fact, the networking opportunities it can provide are among the least publicised but most exciting benefits of all. A good network can have an amazing impact on your life and career. Volunteer for anything from mentoring and befriending to caring for wildlife and animals and local community projects.

## Benefits of volunteering

- Opens up new networks of people.
- Helps develop skills.
- Increases confidence and self-esteem.
- Makes you feel useful and improves your sense of well-being.
- Gives you satisfaction and a sense of achievement.
- Improves your career opportunities.

A Time Bank survey carried out through Reed Executive (an agency who help people find jobs) among 200 of the UK's leading businesses revealed some very interesting information about volunteering:

- 73% of employers would employ candidates with volunteering experience over someone who doesn't.

- 94% of employers believe that volunteering can add to skills.

- 58% say that voluntary work experience can actually be more valuable than experience gained in paid employment.

- 94% of employees who volunteered to learn new skills had benefited either by getting their first job, improving their salary or being promoted.

Check out volunteering possibilities on your university website or look at the ones below for options available to you. You don't have to devote masses of your time but you do have to show commitment and enthusiasm. If you are looking for volunteering opportunities in your area, go to the government website www.direct.gov.uk/homeandcommunity and click on the volunteering link.

Alternatively, V Inspired offers projects for people aged 16-25. You can visit the website at www.vinspired.com.

# Summing Up

Studying at university isn't just about gaining knowledge in your specific subject, it's a whole life experience and you need to make the most of all the opportunities available to you. Try to make any work experience relevant with transferable skills which will stand you in good stead for the future.

When you are applying for jobs, employers will look at all the extra curricula activities on your CV. Playing sport for a university team or being involved in the drama or choral society all add weight to your personal qualities.

Volunteering in whatever capacity is an excellent way to draw attention to your CV and make you more attractive to potential employers. Giving something back to community brings personal gains too. Make every opportunity count!

'Studying at university isn't just about gaining knowledge in your specific subject, it's a whole life experience and you need to make the most of all the opportunities available to you.'

# Help List

## National Union of Students (NUS)

Tel: 0871 221 8221

www.nus.org.uk

While you are in the sixth form you can apply to join the National Union of Students and as an Associate Member you will be able to receive a student discount card called Extra. This will give you all sorts of discounts on a range of services and products from travel and books to clothes and food. You'll also have the opportunity to enter competitions and have access to advice on anything from travel to careers. The card costs £10 and an application form can be downloaded from the website.

## Studentguru.co.uk

www.studentguru.co.uk

This website provides lots of information on all kinds of student related issues. You can get advice on everything from food and accomodation to jobs and money.

## The Student Zone

www.thestudentzone.com

This is an international student community – meet other students, find out about the latest discounts on offer for students, get advice about jobs, graduate and gap year information and competitions. You can easily keep up with the latest student news. Enter the details of your university in the search tab and you will be linked up to your university's profile – you'll find details of local jobs, gigs and the latest discounts.

## UCAS

www.ucas.ac.uk

Not only does this site contain all the information you'll need for applying to university, you also be able to find information on funding, learning to budget and balancing work and study. There's even a budget calculator.

# For students with disabilities

## Skill: National Bureau for Students with Disabilities

www.skill.org.uk

A national charity promoting opportunities for young people and adults with any kind of impairment in post-16 education, training and employment. There are also lots of links to other useful websites.

# Health and wellbeing

## Brook

Tel: 0808 802 1234 (helpline)

www.brook.org.uk

Brook is a registered charity and has 40 years of experience in delivering professional advice. It provides free and confidential sexual health information for young people under 25. All advice is given by properly trained medical staff.

## Embarrassingproblems.com

www.embarrassingproblems.com

This website is provided by Health Press Limited. It provides lots of straightforward information on a range of personal health issues, including sexual health. There's also information on visiting doctors and clinics.

## Netdoctor

www.netdoctor.co.uk

This is a website where you can check out symptoms and health problems and get useful advice on all aspects of your own lifestyle and wellbeing.

## NHS Direct

Tel: 0845 4647 (helpline)

www.nhsdirect.nhs.uk

NHS Direct offers 24-hour health information and advice from a nurse. You can visit the website to find your nearest GP surgery.

## Nightline

www.nightline.niss.ac.uk
Run by students for students, Nightline offers anonymous and confidential support and information. Visit the website to find your local service.

## R U Thinking?

Tel: 0800 28 29 30
www.ruthinking.co.uk
A site delivering sexual facts and information. As well as visiting the website, you can call the free helpline for confidential advice.

## Samaritans

Tel: 08457 90 90 90
www.samaritans.org.uk
A registered charity offering a 24-hour service for emotional support.

## Students Against Depression

www.studentdepression.org
An excellent place to start if you are feeling depressed or are worried about a friend who is showing signs of depression. There are sections on how depression works, putting it into context, self-help strategies for tackling the problem, as well as information on getting help and support.

## Surgery Door

www.surgerydoor.co.uk
This is a website where you can find information on all aspects of healthy living. You can even get advice on what to do in an emergency and tips on healthy eating. There's also a facility that enables you to search for support groups in your area.

# Financial information for students

## AbeBooks

www.abebooks.co.uk
A website which enables you to search through thousands of booksellers for new and used books. It's good for finding your reading list on a budget.

## Money Saving Expert

www.moneysavingexpert.com
Free financial advice from money saving expert Martin Lewis. This website alerts you to two-for-one restaurant offers, theatre and cinema deals, as well as magazine giveaways.

## Money Supermarket

Tel: 0845 345 5708 (customer services)
www.moneysupermarket.com
A website which enables you to compare prices on just about anything: insurance, mobile phones, travel, motoring, gas and electricity. The website ensures that you are always getting the best value for your money.

## Scholarship search

www.scholarship-search.org.uk
Scholarship search enables you to see if you are eligible for a scholarship and view advice on budget planning and loan repayment. You can search by subject or organisation and can email enquiries via the website.

## Student Beans

www.studentbeans.com
A useful website providing students with money off deals and free vouchers.

## Student Finance

**Student Finance England**
Tel: 0845 607 7577
www.direct.gov.uk/studentfinance

The helpline is available Monday to Friday from 8am-8pm and Saturday and Sunday from 9am-5.30pm.

**Student Finance NI**

Tel: 0845 600 0662

www.studentfinanceni.co.uk

The helpline is available Monday to Friday from 8am-8pm and Saturday and Sunday from 9am-5.30pm.

**Scotland Student Awards Agency for Scotland (SAAS)**

Tel: 0845 111 1711

www.student-support-saas.gov.uk

The helpline is available every day from 8am-5pm (4.30pm on Fridays). However, from early June to mid-October it is available every day from 8am-6pm (4.30pm on Fridays).

**Student Finance Wales**

Tel: 0845 602 8845

www.studentfinancewales.co.uk

The helpline is available Monday to Friday from 8am-8pm and Saturday from 9am-1pm. It is closed on Sundays.

These are official websites for applying for student finance. They administer the payment of financial support for students, incorporating the whole process, from promotion and assessment to payment and collection.

# Insurance

## Endsleigh Insurance

Tel: 0800 028 3571 (general enquiries)

www.endsleigh.co.uk

Endsleigh Insurance is the only insurance company recommended by the NUS. You can apply online or by telephone for travel insurance or to cover any of your possessions. Many of their services are specially tailored to meet students' needs.

# Travel

## Megabus

Tel: 0900 160 0900 (ticket line)
www.megabus.com
Megabus enables you to search for low cost inter city travel using the quick 'search and buy' facility.

## National Express

www.nationalexpress.com
A leading website where you can buy train, coach or bus tickets.

## National Rail

www.nationalrail.co.uk
This website is the official source for UK train times and fares. The site is easy to use and delivers all the information you need to plan your journey at the click of a mouse.

## Stagecoach Unirider

www.buymyunirider.com
Stagecoach Unirider provides student passes for travel within certain cities. Check the site to see if your university city is included – you could end up saving a small fortune on your travel expenses!

## Student Railcard

www.16-25railcard.co.uk
A website offering 16-25-year-olds the chance to apply for a railcard. If you buy one, you get one third off all your rail fare.

## The Train Line

www.thetrainline.com
A good website to search for cheap rail fares quickly and easily.

# Accommodation

## Accomodation for Students

www.accommodationforstudents.com
A search engine for student accommodation, student houses and flats. Check out the notice board for the latest vacancies. You can also read feedback about landlords and compare rent costs.

## Homes for Students

www.homesforstudents.co.uk
This website allows you to quickly and easily search for student housing anywhere in the UK. You can also use the 'search for flatmates' facility to find other students to share housing with.

# Food and Nutrition

## BBC Food

www.bbc.co.uk/food/news_and_events/events_student1.shtml
This BBC website provides information on food and cooking for new students. There are also smart shopping tips, budget advice and recipes to try.

## Recipes 4 Us

www.recipes4us.co.uk
The student section on this website provides lots of different cooking ideas and advice for cooking to a budget.

## Studentcook.co.uk

www.studentcook.co.uk
Student Cook was formed to offer a unique reference point on student cooking for all occasions and budgets. The website Includes tips on preparing, cooking, eating, storing and shopping for food. Information on shopping to a budget and healthy eating is included.

## Student Recipes

www.studentrecipes.com
This website provides lots of different recipes posted by students for students. They are all tasty and budget friendly! You can even get the latest recipes sent to your Twitter account if you have one.

## Yumyum.com

www.yumyum.com/student
This is a free recipe website for everyday cooks, including information for students. It contains lots of useful tips and advice on cooking tasty meals.

# Book List

***Applying to University – The Essential Guide***
By Anne Coates, Need2Know, Peterborough, Revised Edition 2009.

***Find Your Focus Zone***
By Lucy Jo Palladino, Simon and Schuster, New York, 2008.

***Sexually Transmitted Infections – The Essential Guide***
By Nicolette Heaton-Harris, Need2Know, Peterborough, 2008.

***Student Cookbook – Healthy Eating – The Essential Guide***
By Ester Davies, Need2Know, Peterborough, 2008.

***The Food Doctor Supereating***
By Ian Marber, Quadrille, London, 2008.

 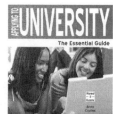 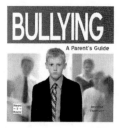